SUSAN HAYWARD
MALCOLM COHAN

bag
of
Jewels

IN TUNE BOOKS

IN-TUNE BOOKS
PO BOX 193
AVALON NSW 2107
AUSTRALIA

First published in September 1988
Revised edition March 1989
2nd Revised edition June 1991

BAG OF JEWELS
Copyright © 1987
by Susan Hayward & Malcolm Cohan
All rights reserved.

Quotations Calligraphy by Yvonne Meani
Jacket Calligraphy by Dave Wood
Endpapers by Margo Snape

Produced by Mandarin Offset, HK.

ISBN 0 9590439 5 O

By the same author
A GUIDE FOR THE ADVANCED SOUL   1985   09590439-O-X
BEGIN IT NOW   1987   09590439-1-8

INTERNATIONAL DISTRIBUTORS:

AUST   *Harper Collins*
UK   *Ashgrove Books, Bath*
NZ   *Lothian Books, Auckland*
USA   *Bookpeople, New Leaf,*
       DeVorss & Co, Ingrams

Foreword

Flowing with the Universe.
Being a channel for it's energy.
Not judging another's path.
Celebrating this gift of life.
Doing only what you love and
Taking the risk to do it
Owning your reality.
Knowing life is fleeting
   and must be lived now!

Seeing yourself as a unique Being
and following your own inner voice -
these are the Jewels we were given
as we worked with this book.

We hope you may be inspired
to live life and know each new
experience is a precious Jewel.

Love.
Susan & Malcolm

Stop freewheeling, get into gear,
and do something with your life.
There are many avenues to
explore, so why not explore them?
Never be afraid to step out into
the unknown, into the new.
Do it fearlessly, always expecting
the very best as you do so.

EILEEN CADDY

Everything is out there waiting for you. All you have to do is walk up and declare yourself in. No need for permission. You just need courage to say, "Include me". Providing you have the energy to pull it off you can do what you like. And the Universal Law, being impartial, will be only too delighted to deliver.

STUART WILDE

80% of success
is just showing up.

WOODY ALLEN

The rich substance of the
Universe is yours to do with
as you wish.
Why settle for so little in life
when you can have so much,
just by daring to be different
in your thinking.

CATHERINE PONDER

When you die and go to heaven
our Maker is not going to ask,
"Why didn't you discover the
cure for such and such? Why
didn't you become the Messiah?"
The only question we will be
asked in that precious moment is
"Why didn't you become you?"

ELIE WIESEL

*People who deliberate fully
before they take a step
will spend their lives
on one leg.*

ANTHONY de MELLO

If you must begin
 then go all the way, because if
 you begin and quit the
 unfinished business you have
 left behind will haunt you
 for all of time.
 The path is like getting
 onto a train that you
 cannot get off.
    You ride on and on.
                    TRUNGPA RINPOCHE

It is not because things
are difficult
that we do not dare;
It is because we do not dare
that they are difficult.

SENECA

*Every man takes the limits
of his own field of vision,
for the limits of the world.*

ARTHUR SCHOPENHAUER

What you love is a sign
from your higher self
of what you are to do.

SANYANA ROMAN

What would it be like if you
lived each day, each breath,
as a work of art in progress?
Imagine that you are a
Masterpiece unfolding,
every second of every day
a work of art taking form
with every breath.

THOMAS CRUM

Whether you think you can
or whether you
think you can't -
you are right.

HENRY FORD

Until thought is linked with purpose, there is no intelligent accomplishment. With the majority, the bark of thought is allowed to drift upon the ocean of life. A man should conceive of a legitimate purpose in his heart, and set out to accomplish it.

JAMES ALLEN

Decree a thing
and it shall be
established
unto thee.

JOB 22:28

Each time you complete an act of creation, you focus a life force. And since life begets life, this energy seeks to enlarge its expression through new creation. In the stage of completion, your being is ready for another act of creation.

ROBERT FRITZ

It is the greatest
   of all mistakes
      to do nothing because you
         can only do a little.
            Do what you can.

SYDNEY SMITH

Life was never meant
to be a struggle
just a gentle progression
from one point to another,
much like walking through
a valley on a sunny day.

STUART WILDE

Be gentle with yourself.
If you will not be your own
unconditional friend,
who will be?
If you are playing an opponent
and you are also opposing
yourself — you are going to
be outnumbered.

DAN MILLMAN

Whatever you are doing
love yourself for doing it.

THADDEUS GOLAS

I learned that
nothing is impossible
when we follow our
inner guidance,
even when it's direction
may threaten us
by reversing our
usual logic.

GERALD JAMPOLSKY

The miracle comes quietly
into the mind
that stops an instant
and is still.

A COURSE IN
MIRACLES

Most decisions, possibly all, have already been made on some deeper level and my going through a reasoning process to arrive at them seems at least redundant. The question, "What do 1 want to do?" may be a fearful reaction to the subconscious decision 1 have already made.

HUGH PRATHER

The worst thing
you can possibly do
is worry about
what you could
have done.

LICHTENBERG

We are all on a spiral path.
No growth takes place in a
straight line. There will be
setbacks along the way... There
will be shadows, but they will be
balanced by patches of light and
fountains of joy as we grow and
progress. Awareness of the pattern
is all you need to sustain you
along the way...

KRISTIN ZAMBUCKA

Be willing to do what
your soul directs you to do
if you want to create what
you are asking for.

SANYANA ROMAN

Everyone finds their own
doorway to walk through.
Each doorway you walk
through will bring you into
a new space of Being.
As you create new spaces
to walk into, stand a
moment in the doorway

and review the scene behind you
then turn and for a moment be
awe inspired with the wonder
of the new space you have
created to play into.
    At least give yourself
    that moment.

GITA BELLIN

In a world where death
is the hunter, my friend,
there is no time for
regrets or doubts.
There is only time
for decisions.

CARLOS CASTANEDA

You have got to know what
it is you want! Or someone is
going to sell you a bill of goods
somewhere along the line that
will do irreparable damage
to your self-esteem, your sense
of worth, and your stewardship
of talents that God gave you.

RICHARD NELSON BOLLES

You are a child of the Universe
no less than the trees
and the stars
you have a right to be here.
And whether or not
it is clear to you
no doubt the Universe is
unfolding as
it should.

MAX EHRMANN

Be a football to Time and chance,
the more kicks the better,
so that you inspect
the whole game and
know its utmost law.

RALPH WALDO EMERSON

The only thing
that makes life possible
is permanent
intolerable

uncertainty:
the joy of not knowing
what comes next.

URSULA LEGUIN

When you are pushed
   pull.
When you are pulled
   push.
Find the natural course
and bend with it,
then you join with
nature's power.

DAN MILLMAN

To try is to risk failure.
But risk must be taken because
the greatest hazard of life is to
risk nothing. The person who
risks nothing does nothing,
has nothing, is nothing.
He may avoid suffering and
sorrow, but he simply cannot
learn, feel, change, grow, live,
and love.

LEO BUSCAGLIA

Life's a pretty precious
   and wonderful thing.
You can't sit down and
let it lap around you...
you have to plunge into it,
you have to dive through it.

KYLE CRICHTON

What is right for one soul
may not be right for another.
It may mean having to stand
on your own and do something
strange in the eyes of others.
But do not be daunted.
Do whatever it is because
you know within it is
right for you..

EILEEN CADDY

Conformity leads to mediocrity.
If the individual is to grapple
with life, it's intricacies,
it's miseries and sudden
demands, he must be
infinitely pliable,
and therefore free of theories
and particular patterns
of thought.

KRISHNAMURTI

Live
   as you will have
      wished to have lived
         when you are dying.

GELLERT

I wish I'd drunk
more champagne.

Last words of
MAYNARD KEYNES,
Economist

The goal is
to be an instrument of God.
The more confident we are,
the more intuition works
through us.

                    PAUL NEARY

Allow life
to be the theatre of God,
in which what seems
appropriate and
necessary in your case
will be accomplished
spontaneously.
You must trust the process
of your own life.

HEART-MASTER DA LOVE-ANANDA

Find inner peace and you will
have endless energy –
the more you give,
the more you receive.
After you have found
your calling,
you work easily
and joyously.
You never get tired.

PEACE PILGRIM

Nothing on earth
can overcome
an absolutely
non-resistant
person.

FLORENCE SCOVEL SHINN

In all activities of life
from trivial to important
the secret of efficiency
lies in an ability to
combine two seemingly
incompatible states –
a state of maximum
activity and a state
of maximum relaxation.

ALDOUS HUXLEY

There is no point in work
unless it absorbs you
like an absorbing game.
If it doesn't absorb you,
if it's never any fun,
Don't do it.

D.H. LAWRENCE

Simplicity is the highest quality
of expression. It is that quality to
which art comes in its supreme
moments. It makes the final
stage of growth. It is the rarest,
as it is the most precious,
result which men secure
in their self-training.

LAO TZU

In the beginners mind
there are many possibilities.
But in the expert's
there are few.

SHUNRYU SUZUKI

In alchemy it is stated that whenever we define the space for which we are responsible, everything is given us within that space. It is as if the whole Universe comes down and sits at our feet... ready to be used for God's Plan on Earth.

RESHAD FEILD

How soon
will you realise that
the only thing you don't have
is the direct experience
that there's nothing
you need
that you
don't have?

KEN KEYES

Don't exclude yourself...
 from precious moments
  warm encounters
  beautiful attitudes
  majestic discoveries
  flowing intimacies
  sensory development
for these are the jewels placed
in the crown of your destiny.

WALTER RINDER

Some people
walk in the rain.
Others just get wet.

ROGER MILLER

We grow great by dreams.
All big men are dreamers.
They see things in the soft haze
of a spring day or in the red
fire of a long winter's evening.
Some of us let our dreams die,
but others nourish and protect
them, nurse them through bad
days till they bring them to
sunshine and light.

WOODROW WILSON

*Why not go out on a limb?
That's where the fruit is.*

WILL ROGERS

Often people attempt to live their lives backwards: they try to have more things or more money, in order to do more of what they want, so they will be happier. The way it actually works is the reverse. You must first _be_ who you really are, then, _do_ what you need to do, in order to _have_ what you want.

MARGARET YOUNG

Sometimes
the only way for me to find out
what it is I want to do
is go ahead and do
something.
Then the moment I start
to act, my feelings
become clear.

HUGH PRATHER

Feel the fear...
And do it anyway.

SUSAN JEFFERS

Faith
is the bird
that feels the light
when the dawn
is still dark.

RABINDRANATH TAGORE

Power comes from understanding that wherever others are is where they need to be, and whatever they are doing is for their highest growth, and you should not judge it. Totally accepting other people's reality invigorates your own progress, because judgement holds you back to the baser physical levels.

STUART WILDE

You cannot know
 your own perfection
  until you have honoured
   all those who were created
   like you.

A COURSE IN
MIRACLES

The reason why
birds can fly
and we can't
is simply that
they have
perfect faith,
for to have faith
is to have wings.

JAMES M. BARRIE

*Never
place limits
on yourself.
Just be free
at all costs!*

PELEI

Eliminate something superfluous
from your life. Break a habit.
Do something that makes
you feel insecure.
Carry out an action
with complete attention
and intensity as if it
were your last.

PIERRO FERRUCCI

He who isn't busy
being born
is busy dying.

BOB DYLAN

We outgrow people, places, and things as we unfold. We may be saddened when old friends say their piece and leave our lives... but let them go. They were at a different stage... and looking in a different direction.

KRISTIN ZAMBUCKA

Even a happy life
cannot be without
a measure of darkness,
and the word "happiness"
would lose it's meaning
if it were not balanced
by sadness.

CARL JUNG

At some stages you will
experience a plateau – as if
everything had stopped.
This is a hard point in the
journey. Know that once the
process has started it doesn't
stop; it only appears to stop
from where you are looking.

RAM DASS

When one door closes
another opens.
Expect that new door
to reveal even greater
wonders and glories
and surprises.
Feel yourself grow
with every experience.
And look for the reason
for it.

EILEEN CADDY

To be happy
one must risk
unhappiness.
To live fully one must
risk death and accept
its ultimate decision.

JUDD MARMOR

Death is a very positive force because it tells me I have limited time. No one will get out of this world alive. But there are some of us who actually believe we will. We act as if we have forever! "I've always wanted to climb a mountain.. I'll do it tomorrow" You may not.

LEO BUSCAGLIA

We achieve a sense of self
from what we do for ourselves
and how we develop our
capacities. If all your efforts
have gone into developing others,
you're bound to feel empty.

TAKE YOUR TURN NOW.

ROBIN NORWOOD

A relationship should not suppress our adventure or suppress the speed with which we learn the lessons that are there for us to learn.

STEWART EMERY

'The great essentials to
happiness in this life are
something to do
something to love
and something to
hope for.

JOSEPH ADDISON

One oral utterance, which
boldly states how you want
your life to be, is worth more
than a dozen books read or
lectures attended.
Spoken words describing
the good you want, help you
to claim it and release it
into your own life quickly.

CATHERINE PONDER

Lao Tzu fell asleep and
dreamt he was a butterfly.
Upon wakening he asked,
"Am I a man who
has just been dreaming
that he was a butterfly?
Or a sleeping butterfly
now dreaming he is
a man?"

LAO TZU

You are in physical existence
to learn and understand that
your energy, translated into
feelings, thoughts and emotions,
causes all experience.
There are no exceptions.

SETH

Love who you are and what
you are and what you do.
Laugh at yourself and at life,
and nothing can touch you.
It's all temporary anyway.
Next lifetime you will do it
differently anyway, so why
not do it differently now?

LOUISE L. HAY

The past existed in
multitudinous ways.
You only experienced one
probable past. By changing
this past in your mind now,
in your present, you can change
not only it's nature, but also
it's effect, and not only upon
yourself but upon others.

SETH

To forgive is the highest,
   most beautiful form of love.
      In return, you will receive
         untold peace
            and happiness.

ROBERT MULLER

Nothing can hurt you
unless you give it
the power to do so.

A COURSE IN
MIRACLES

If you are
never scared
or embarrassed
or hurt,
it means you never take
chances.

JULIA SOUL

Change and growth take place
when a person has
risked himself,
and dares to become
involved in experimenting
with his own life.

HERBET OTTO

Never waste time and energy wishing you were somewhere else, doing something else. Accept your situation and realise you are where you are, doing what you are doing, for a very specific reason. Realise that nothing is by chance, that you have certain lessons to learn and that the situation you are in has been given to you to enable you to learn those lessons as quickly as possible, so that you can move onward and upward along this spiritual path.

EILEEN CADDY

You are here for a purpose.
There is no duplicate of you
in the whole wide world.
There never has been
There never will be.
You were brought here now
to fill a certain need.
Take time to
think that over.

LOU AUSTIN

The purpose of life is to matter—
to count
to stand for something
to have it make some
difference that
we lived at all.

LEO ROSTEN

To enter into an
unpredictable situation
and accept it openly
is to flow with it's energy,
be augmented in your
own energy and relax it's
stresses and tensions
accordingly.

JOSEPH CHILTON PEARCE

A crisis event
often explodes
the illusions
that anchor
our lives.

ROBERT VENINGA

Notice the difference between
what happens when a man
says to himself
"I have failed three times",
and what happens
when he says
"I am a failure".

The more you are willing
to trust yourself, and take risks
to follow your inner guidance,
the more money you will have.
The Universe will pay you
to be yourself and do what you
really love.

SHAKTI GAWAIN

Go and learn from your teachers and your religions until you are bored. Then seek the answer that feels right within your soul. When the truth feels right, that is your soul rejoicing, because the grandest truth is unlimited freedom ~ whatever allows you to experience any truth you desire.

RAMTHA

No spirit guide
teacher or
philosophy
is higher
than you!
There is nothing higher
than you!

MARSHALL N. LEVER

The things you believe in are
the baggage you carry with you
in your life. The true sage
believes in nothing, other than
the sacredness of all things.
He lives in spontaneity of energy.
He defends nothing nor judges
anything. His world is eternal and

infinite, he sees beauty in all things and he accepts the ways of man, including restriction and strife. He knows that without constraints there would be no challenges.

STUART WILDE

Physical reality is the biggest horror movie of all, and you know how we love horror movies. If the Universe as we see it from our vibration level is illusory, than that's all the more reason for enjoying it, and loving it, instead of getting freaked out by it.

THADDEUS GOLAS

Perception
  is a mirror not a fact.
    And what I look on
      is my state of mind,
        reflected outward.

A COURSE IN
MIRACLES

You have no idea
of the tremendous release
and deep peace that comes
from meeting yourself
and your brothers
totally without
judgement.

A COURSE IN
MIRACLES

Love it the way it is!
The way you see the world
depends entirely
on your own vibration.
When your vibration changes
the whole world
will look different.
It's like those days when
everyone seems smiling at you
because you feel happy.

THADDEUS GOLAS

The Universal Law is impartial.
It will give you anything you believe.
It will throw you garbage or roses
depending on the energy you put
in. You are the one in charge, and
you must accept that and stand
alone. If you think God is coming
down to fix things for you, forget
it. God is out playing golf.

STUART WILDE

I never give out my zodiac sign.
Do you honestly think I can be
pushed around by a planet?
Good heavens,
   your divine nature
   is always free.

PEACE PILGRIM

I never came upon any
of my discoveries
through the process
of rational thinking.

ALBERT EINSTEIN

Feelings are
the holiest force
in the Universe
(they are the only
reason for life),
and the feeling of love
is the holiest of the holy.

TERRY COLE-WHITTAKER

We are each of us angels
with only one wing.
And we can fly only
by embracing
each other.

LUCIANO de CRESCENZO

Falling in love is actually a
powerful experience of feeling
the Universe move through you.
The other person has become
a channel for you, a catalyst
that triggers you to open up
to the love, beauty and
compassion within.

SHAKTI GAWAIN

To be sure of winning
    invent your own game
    (and never tell any
    other player the rules).

ASHLEIGH BRILLIANT

You never live so fully
as when you gamble
with your own life.

ANTHONY de MELLO

Once you make the fundamental
choice to be the predominant
creative force in your life,
any approach you choose
to take for your own growth
and development can work,
and you will be especially
attracted to those approaches
which will work particularly
well for you.

ROBERT FRITZ

You don't have to suffer
continual chaos
in order to grow.

JOHN C. LILLY

Fear is
not of the present
but only of past and future
which does not exist.

A COURSE IN
MIRACLES

The major way
to conquer fear
is to make a
decision.

RESHAD FEILD

At bottom,
  every man knows well enough
  that he is a unique human
  being, only once on this earth;
  and by no extraordinary
  chance will such a
  marvellously picturesque
  piece of diversity in unity
  as he is, ever be put
  together a second time.

NIETZCHE

Find your own unique
   expression of the Godforce.
    Don't mimic
     for it is already
     too late.

         Create anew.

                GITA BELLIN

I am me.
In all the world there is
no one else exactly like me.
There are persons who have
parts like me, but no one who
adds up exactly like me.
Therefore, everything that
comes out of me is authentically
mine because I alone chose it.

VIRGINIA SATIR

Your Goal
is to find out
Who You Are.

A COURSE IN
MIRACLES

This life, master, was not
created to be a prison.
It was designed to be a
platform for creativity
and expression that is
colorful and challenging,
and upon which you have
many interludes and
adventures - but always
because they bring you joy.

RAMTHA

This is your life and nobody
is going to teach you, no book,
no guru. Learn from yourself,
not from books. It is an endless
thing, a fascinating thing and
when you learn about your
self from yourself, out of that
learning wisdom comes. Then you
can live a most extraordinary,
happy, beautiful life. Right?

KRISHNAMURTI

A love of excellence makes the small thing a source of satisfaction.
On the inner planes, thorough work creates archetypes that ensoul the object as long as it exists.

FLOWER A. NEWHOUSE

Do what you love...
the money will follow.

MARSHA SINETAR

Nothing
is more dangerous
than an idea.
When it is the
only one you have.

EMILE CHARTIER

If you are seeking
creative ideas,
go out walking.
Angels whisper to a man
when he goes for a walk.

RAYMOND INMON .

Imagination . . .
is one of the motivating agencies
that helps transform your
beliefs into physical experience.
To dislodge unsuitable beliefs
and establish new ones,
the proper use of imagination
can then propel ideas in any
direction you desire.

SETH

If you have built
   castles in the air,
   your work need not be lost;
   that is where they should be.
Now put the foundations
   under them!

HENRY DAVID THOREAU

It is time to show
the strength of water,
and flow away.
To stand is to be crushed,
but to flow out is
to gather new strength.

MARGE PIERCY

Instead of seeing
the rug being pulled
from under us,
we can learn to dance
on a shifting carpet.

THOMAS CRUM

The only aspect of time that is eternal is now.

A COURSE IN
MIRACLES

Let the clock and the earth
do their own thing ...
Let the comings and goings
of life continue ...
But YOU stay HERE and NOW.
This exercise is to bring
you to the Eternal Present
where it all is.

RAM DASS

The higher one climbs
on the spiritual ladder,
the more he will grant
others their own freedom
and give less interference
to another's state of
consciousness.

PAUL TWITCHELL

Those who know
do not say.
Those who say
do not know.

LAO TZU

There is NO RIGHT WAY.
There is only THE WAY that
is best for those who find their
own way, the way that helps
them become a better
spiritual being.

PELEI

Eat and carouse with Bacchus
or munch dry bread
with Jesus.
But don't sit down
without one of
the gods.

D.H. LAWRENCE

Killing the Budda on the road means destroying the hope that anything outside ourselves can be our master. No one is bigger than anyone else. There are no mothers and fathers for grown-ups, only sisters and brothers.

SHELDON KOPP

Any path
　is only a path.
There is no affront
　　to oneself or others
　　　　in dropping it
if that is what
　　your heart tells you.

CARLOS CASTANEDA

The most beautiful thing
we can experience
is the mystery.

ALBERT EINSTEIN

Chaos demands to
be recognised
and experienced
before letting itself be converted
into a new order.

HERMAN HESSE

It is only an illusion
that you do not have
what you want.

SANYANA ROMAN

The use of money
is all the advantage
there is in having
money.

BENJAMIN FRANKLIN

There is in addition to the
"up and down" cycles,
an "in and out" cycle.
That is, there are stages at which
we feel pulled into inner work
and all you seek is a quiet place
to meditate. Then there are
times when you turn outward
and seek to be involved in the

marketplace. Both of these cycles
are part of one's sadhana.
For what happens in the
marketplace helps you in
meditation and what happens
in meditation helps you
participate in the marketplace
without attachment.

RAM DASS

It is an orderly universe,
and the suffering that comes
to us has a purpose in our lives -
it is trying to teach us something.
We should look for its lesson.

PEACE PILGRIM

The soul
would have
no rainbow,
had the eyes
no tears.

JOHN VANCE CHENEY

When a little bubble of joy
appears in your sea of
consciousness take hold of it
and keep expanding it.
Meditate on it and it will
grow larger. Keep puffing
at the bubble until it breaks
it's confining walls and
becomes a sea of joy.

PARAMAHANSA YOGANANDA

Life kisses us on both cheeks
Day and morn
But laughs at our deeds
Eve and dawn.

KAHLIL GIBRAN

Your health is bound to be affected if day after day you say the opposite of what you feel, if you grovel before what you dislike and rejoice at what brings you nothing but misfortune.

DR. ZHIVAGO

Life
is an opportunity
and not an obligation.

THE TAO OF LEADERSHIP

You see everything depends
upon the psychological
headquarters from which
we live.
"Where am I living from?"
Ask yourself that question.
If you don't like your headquarters,
you can move any time you like.
Break away. Don't tell anyone

about it. Others will either smile tolerantly or mouth sanctimonious babble. Make your escape plans in secret. Never mind if you lose certain friends, you will find others who also have dared. They will be ten-thousand times more valuable to you.

VERNON HOWARD

Fear:

The best way out
is through.

HELEN KELLER

Since everything is
but an apparition,
perfect in being what it is,
having nothing to do with
good or bad,
acceptance or rejection
one may well burst out
into laughter.

LONG CHEN PA

Don't surrender
your individuality,
which is your greatest agent
of power, to the customs and
conventionalities that have
got their life from the great
mass...

Do you want to be a power in
the world? Then be yourself.

RALPH WALDO TRINE

Being myself includes
taking risks with myself,
taking risks on new behaviour,
trying new ways of
"being myself",
so that I can see
how it is
I want to be.

HUGH PRATHER

Life is like a motor car.
A motor car can be used
to travel great heights.
But most people lie in
front of it, allow it to
drive over them, then
blame it for the accident.

ANTHONY de MELLO

80% of all deaths may actually be suicides. Persons who lack curiosity about life, who are guilt-ridden and depressed and conditioned by parental example, are all too willing, subconsciously, to cooperate with and attract disease, accident and violence.

TOM ROBBINS

Imagine you only have one year to live. What important things would you be doing? How would you be alloting your time to accomplish the most you could? This exercise is one method of going after your priorities.

DENIS WAITLEY

The only way you can live
forever is to love somebody –
then you really leave a gift behind.
When you live that way, as I've
seen with people with physical
illness, you literally have a
choice of when you die.

DR BERNARD SIEGEL, MD

This Saturday,
do something you have wanted
to do for years.
to do for years.
Something
just for yourself.
And repeat this process
once every month.

DENIS WAITLEY

I got the blues
thinking of the future,
so I left off and
made some marmalade.
It's amazing how
it cheers one up
to shred oranges
and scrub the floor.

D.H. LAWRENCE

The more you talk about it,
and the more you think
about it, the further
from it you go.
Stop talking,
Stop thinking,
and there is nothing you
will not understand.

SENG-TS'AN

A person knowing
the power of his word,
becomes very careful
in his conversation.
He only has to watch the
reaction of his words
to know that they
"do not return void".

FLORENCE SCOVEL SHINN

What we vividly imagine,
ardently desire,
enthusiastically act upon,
must inevitably
come to pass.

COLIN P. SISSON

A rockpile
   ceases to be a rockpile
   the moment a single man
   contemplates it,
   bearing within him
       the image of
           a cathedral.

ANTOINE de SAINT-EXUPERY

Que sera, sera
   is a lovely song,
      but a lousy philosophy.
Nothing worthwhile
   was ever accomplished
      by anybody who met life
      with a shrug.
Instead your motto should
   be: "Que quiero sera"
      whatever I will, will be.

EDWIN C. BLISS

Any idea
    seriously entertained
        tends to bring about
            the realisation
            of itself.

JOSEPH CHILTON PEARCE

The greatest achievement was
at first and for a time a dream.
The oak sleeps in the acorn.
The bird waits in the egg.
And in the highest vision
of a soul, a waking angel stirs.
Dreams are the seedlings of
realities.

JAMES ALLEN

Believing is one thing,
    doing another.
Many talk like the sea but
their lives are stagnant marshes.
Others raise their heads
above the mountain tops,
while their souls cling to
the dark walls of caves.

KAHLIL GIBRAN

How was Einstein able to conceive the Theory of Relativity? He said the one crucial thing that helped him was his ability to visualise: "what would it be like to be riding on the end of a light beam?"

ANTHONY ROBBINS

Cluttered closets
   mean a cluttered mind.
As you clean the closet,
say to yourself,
"I am cleaning the
   closets of my mind".
The Universe loves
   symbolic gestures.

LOUISE L. HAY

Whoever I am
and whatever I am doing,
some kind excellence
is within my reach.

JOHN W. GARDENER

I saw life through the
eyes of a child as I watched
him clean his boat
before putting it into the lake.
We can learn from children.

WALTER RINDER

Logical thinking cannot
yield us any knowledge of
the empirical world;
all knowledge of reality
starts from experience
and ends in it.
Propositions arrived at by
purely logical means are
completely empty of reality.

ALBERT EINSTEIN

What comes from the heart
touches the heart.

DON SIBET

The union of feminine and masculine energies within the individual is the basis of creation. Female intuition plus male action is creativity. Put the female in the guiding position - this is her natural function. She is your intuition,

the door to your higher intelligence.
The true function of the male
energy is absolute clarity,
directness and a passionate
strength based on what the
universe, coming through
your female, tells you.

SHAKTI GAWAIN

The meeting of
two personalities is like
the contact of two
chemical substances:
if there is any reaction
both are transformed.

CARL JUNG

A partner will bring up
    all your patterns.
Don't avoid relationships:
    they are the best seminar
        in town.
The truth is
    that your partner
        is your guru.

SONDRA RAY

Everything has its wonders
even darkness and silence.
I learn that
whatever state
I may be in
therein
to be
content.

HELEN KELLER

Whenever we communicate
with each other correctly
there is an exchange
of energy.

RESHAD FEILD

Humility
is the acceptance
of the possibility
that someone else can teach you
something else you do not know
about yourself.
Conversely,
pride and arrogance,
close the door of the mind.

ARTHUR DEIKMAN

Suppose you never heard anything by accident? Suppose there was a reason behind everything everyone is saying to you? Suppose there was only one Mind, the Universal Mind, and it was doing nothing all day but speaking to you. Would this affect the way you heard criticism?

TERRY COLE-WHITTAKER

IF I HAD MY LIFE TO LIVE OVER

I'd like to make more
   mistakes next time.
   I'd relax, I would limber up.
   I would be sillier
      than I have been this trip.
   I would take fewer
      things seriously.

I would take more chances.
I would climb more mountains
and swim more rivers.
I would eat more ice cream
and less beans.
I would perhaps have more
actual troubles, but I'd have
fewer imaginary ones.

You see, I'm one of those people
who live sensibly and sanely
hour after hour, day after day.
Oh, I've had my moments, and if
I had to do it again, I'd have
more of them. In fact, I'd try to
have nothing else. Just moments,
one after the other, instead of
living so many years ahead
of each day.

3.

I've been one of those persons
   who never goes anywhere
   without a thermometer,
   a hot water bottle, a raincoat,
   and a parachute.
If I had to do it again, I would
   travel lighter than I have.

If I had my life to live over,
  I would start barefoot earlier
  in the spring and stay that way
  later in the fall.
  I would go to more dances.
  I would ride more merry-go-rounds.
  I would pick more daisies.

NADINE STAIR

5.

Bibliography

We gratefully acknowledge the following:

A Course in Miracles. *Accept This Gift.* Edited by Frances Vaughan & Roger Walsh. Los Angeles: Jeremy P. Tarcher, Inc. Copyright 1983 by the Foundation for Inner Peace.

Allen, James. *As A Man Thinketh.* California: DeVorss & Company.

Ashley, Nancy. *A Seth Workbook.* NY: Prentice Hall Press, 1987.

Bellin, Gita. *Amazing Grace, Book One.* Sydney: Gita Bellin & Associates. 1987.

Bliss, Edwin C. *Doing It Now.* London: Macdonald & Company, 1983.

Brilliant, Ashley. *Appreciate Me Now* and *Avoid the Rush.* Santa Barbara: Woodbridge Press Publishing Company, 1987.

Buscaglia, Leo F. *Living, Loving & Learning.* NY: Ballantine Books, 1982.

Caddy, Eileen. *Opening Doors Within.* Scotland: Findhorn Press, 1986.

Castaneda, Carlos. *Journey to Ixtlan.* NY: Ballantine Books, 1979.

Cole-Whittaker, Terry. *The Inner Path from Where You Are to Where You Want to Be.* NY: Ballantine Books, 1986.

Crum, Thomas F. *The Magic of Conflict.* NY: Simon & Schuster, 1987.

De Mello, Anthony. *One Minute Wisdom.* NY: Image Books, Doubleday, 1988.

Field, Reshad. *Steps to Freedom.* Vermont: Threshold Publishing, 1983.

Fritz, Robert. *The Path of Least Resistance.* Salem: DMA Inc., 1984.

Gawain, Shakti. *Living In The Light,* with Laurel King. California: Whatever Publishing Inc., 1986.

Gibran, Kahlil. *Spiritual Sayings.* London: William Heinemanm Ltd., 1962.

Golas, Thaddeus. *The Lazy Man's Guide to Enlightenment.* NY: Bantam Books, 1972.

Hay, Louise L. *You Can Heal Your Life.* Santa Monica: Hay House, 1984.

Heart-Master Da Love-Ananda. *Compulsory Dancing.* San Rafael: The Dawn Horse Press, 1978.

Howard, Vernon. *The Mystic Path to Cosmic Power.* NY: Parker Publishing Company, 1967.

Jampolsky, Gerald G. *Love is Letting Go of Fear.* California: Celestial Arts, 1979.

Jeffers, Susan. *Feel the Fear and Do It Anyway.* London: Century Hutchinson, 1987.

Keyes, Ken. *The Handbook to Higher Consciousness.* Kentucky: The Living Love Center, 1975.

Kopp, Sheldon. *If You Meet the Buddha on the Road, Kill Him!* London: Sheldon Press, 1972.

Medhurst, C. Spurgeon. *The Tao-Teh-King Sayings of Lao Tzu.* Illinois: Theosophical Publishing House, 1972.

Millman, Dan. *Way of the Peaceful Warrior.* California: H.J. Kramer Inc., 1980. *The Warrior Athlete.* StillPoint Publishing, New Hampshire, 1979.

Norwood, Robin. *Women Who Love Too Much.* NY Pocket Books, 1985.

Pearce, Joseph Chilton. *The Magical Child.* NY: Bantam Books, by arrangement E.P. Dutton Inc., 1977.

Ponder, Catherine. *Open Your Mind to Receive* and *Dare to Prosper!* LA: DeVorss & Company 1983, both titles.

Prather, Hugh. *Notes to Myself.* NY: Bantam Books. Copyright 1970 Real People Press, Utah.

By the same Author

A Guide For The Advanced Soul. 1984
Begin It Now. 1987

For information on In-Tune Books
availability please write to
P.O. Box 193, Avalon Beach
NSW 2107, Australia

Ram Dass. *Be Here Now.* Tennessee: Hanuman Foundation, 1978.

Ramtha. Edited by Steven Lee Weinburg. Washington: Sovereignty Inc,. 1986.

Ray, Sondra. *Loving Relationships* CA: Celestial Arts, 1980.

Rinder, Walter. *This Time Called Life.* Celestial Arts.

Robbins, Anthony. *Unlimited Power.* NY: Fawcett Columbine. Ballantine Books, 1986.

Roman, Sanyana. *Living With Joy.* CA: HJ Kramer Inc. 1986.

Satir, Virginia. *The Declaration of Self Esteem.*

Shinn, Florence Scovel. *The Game of Life And How To Play It.* CA: Devorss & Company. 1925.

Sinetar, Marsha. *Do What You Love, The Money Will Follow.* NY: Paulist Press, 1987.

Trine, Ralph Waldo. *In Tune With The Infinite.* 1986 Keats Publishing, Inc., Connecticut.

Paul Twitchell, *In My Soul I Free,* page 93. Reprinted by permission of ECKANKAR

Waitley, Denis and Reni L. Witt. *The Joy Of Working* NY: Ballantine Books, and *The Winners Edge,* Copyright© 1980 NY: Berkeley Publishing Group.

Wilde, Stuart. *The Force.* Taos New Mexico: Wisdom Books Inc., 1984. *Life Was Never Meant To Be A Struggle.* White Dove International Inc., 1987.

Zambucka, Kristin. *Ano Ano: The Seed.* Hawaii: Mana Publishing Co.